MW00936421

House Moving Checklists

Preparation for Relocation

Barbara Bruhwiler

3. Edition June 2020

© Barbara Bruhwiler 2015

All rights reserved. No part of this publication may be reproduced, stored in a retrieval system, or transmitted, in any form or by any means, electronic, mechanical, photo-copying, recording or otherwise, without the prior written permission of the author. Brief quotations embodied in critical articles or reviews are permitted.

Although every precaution has been taken in the prepara-tion of this book, the publisher and author assume no responsibility for errors or omissions. Nor is any liability or responsibility assumed for damages from the use of the information contained herein.

Any perceived slight of any individual or organization is purely unintentional.

Every effort has been made to make this eBook as complete and as accurate as possible, but no warranty or fitness is implied. Neither the author nor the publisher assume any responsibility or liability whatsoever on the behalf of the purchaser or reader of these materials. The reader is respon-sible for his or her own actions.

ISBN: 978-1977828897

Table of Content

Introduction:
Miserable and Stressed
for Weeks and Months...

Moving home doesn't have to do this to you.

Yet researchers and psychologists say it is one of the most stressful events in our life.

When you're preparing for moving home a few things are challenging, even a bit scary:

First of all, the sheer amount of what has to be thought of, organized and done is overwhelming.

You find yourself with this niggling voice at the back of your mind, asking again and again: "But didn't you forget something important?"

Second, prioritizing tasks is tough.
What is 'need to do', and what is 'nice to do'? Not only perfectionists find themselves with health-issues from overwork and stress.

Third, timing is a very tricky part of moving.
We don't always see when a certain task needs to be done. Yet timing is extremely important... Pack your bedding too early and you end up sleeping wrapped in bathroom towels

for the next few weeks. Worse even, giving notice to your landlord too late will become a costly overlook.

A little assistance with planning all of this is very much appreciated, right?

It will help you save money, stress and time.

You will gain an easy relocation, peace of mind, time to relax and generally a good time.

This book will help you cut the time you need for the preparation of your relocation in half.

Instead of having you read a 300-page-book, for which you won't have the time anyway, I did the hard work for you and compiled

the perfect Moving Checklists collection:

> All the important tasks are listed

Peace of mind: you won't forget anything.

> With clear priorities

Relax: What is essential is on the *Moving Checklists*. The rest is second priority.

> Following a timeline

Organized: Start with what needs to be done first and work your way towards moving day.

These are the *Moving Checklists* for the preparation of your relocation:

*** More than 2 Months to go – House Moving Checklist

(only in the *International Moving Checklists* collection)

*** 2 Months to go – House Moving Checklist

*** 1 Month to go – House Moving Checklist

*** 3 Weeks to go – House Moving Checklist

*** 1 Week to go – House Moving Checklist

*** Change of Address – House Moving Checklist

There is a collection for people who move abroad and a different collection for the folks who stay within the same country.

You'll find all of these Moving Checklists in this book's two Appendixes (from page 59).

And (something I highly recommend!) you can download all of these Moving Checklists in pdf format from this webpages:

Collection #1: International Moving Checklists collection: **www.tinyUrl.com/IntMovi**

Collection #2: Domestic Moving Checklists collection: **www.tinyUrl.com/MoviDom**

Why do I recommend it?
Because you can print the lists, carry them with you, and tick off what you accomplished!

Plus you'll discover top tips for the preparation of your relocation in this book, many of which you can't find anywhere else. I cut out the 'common sense' advice to make sure this book can be read in less than one hour. Time is precious before your relocation.

Why do I know anything about relocations?

Who am I?

My name is Barbara Bruhwiler. I love to write magazine articles, blog posts and books about the modern mobile, global lifestyle, which I find utterly fascinating.

Between the age of 19 and 39 I moved home about every four years.

Reasons for my relocations included university studies in my home country as well as overseas, my first job, getting married, renovating a centuries old house in Italy, having our first child, accepting an international assignment in South Africa...

Thus it has been quite a few times that I packed up my belongings, sent change of address notes, loaded my boxes, registered with new utilities, collected keys to my new home, and so on.

During these years, I also got to experience a couple of different ways of how moving can be done:

- stuffing my bed & bookshelf into my uncle's mobile home (university)
- renting a truck & ask friends for help (first job)
- having my belongings shipped across the seven seas in a metal cargo container (off to South Africa)

In short: I have a fair bit of personal experience with relocations.

But I hate to spend time on what I *have* to do; I want to do things I *enjoy* (and moving home is not part of the latter, even though I always liked the outcome).

That's why I had to come up with a plan on how to cut the time spent on preparing for relocation in half. This blueprint is in your hands now, for you to use immediately.

As mentioned earlier, I don't want to waste your time, so let's get started:

1

First Things First:
Let's get Organized

And your first step to take when preparing for your relocation is to get yourself perfectly organized.

Download and print all the *Moving Checklists* that accompany this book.

Following the correct timeline, all the steps for preparing your relocation are clearly outlined on the accompanying *Moving Checklists*:

*** More than 2 Months to go – House Moving Checklist

(only in the *International Moving Checklists* collection)

*** 2 Months to go – House Moving Checklist

*** 1 Month to go – House Moving Checklist

*** 3 Weeks to go – House Moving Checklist

*** 1 Week to go – House Moving Checklist

*** Change of Address – House Moving Checklist

Moving overseas

Some of you are moving abroad, which is a bit different from a local relocation.

You'll find the collection of *Moving Checklists* for your international relocation in Appendix 2 (page 85).

Even better, you can download and print them from this website:

www.tinyUrl.com/IntMovi

Moving to a different country adds a few tasks that need to be accomplished before you can unpack your belongings in your new home: you will need to take care of passports, visa, and so on. That's why your lists are a bit different from the *Domestic Moving Checklists* collection.

Moving within your country

Most people relocate within the same country, thus organizing passports, visa and so on is not an issue for them.

Therefore the tasks you need to accomplish for a top preparation of your relocation are slightly different. You'll find your collection of Moving Checklists in Appendix 1 of this book (page 59), or you can download and print them here:

www.tinyUrl.com/MoviDom

2

Take Control
of the Paperwork

Seemingly trivial, but most important: Organize your paperwork for your relocation from the start. Thus you make sure you'll keep on top of it at all times.

You can easily do this in 8 quick steps:

Step # 1: *Relocation Folder*

Open a new folder on your computer called "Relocation Folder".

Step # 2:

Download the collection of *Moving Checklists* that you need through these links:

Collection #1: International Moving Checklists collection: www.tinyUrl.com/IntMovi

Collection #2: Domestic Moving Checklists collection: www.tinyUrl.com/MoviDom

Step # 3:

Save each list you downloaded to your *Relocation Folder*.

Step # 4: Moving File

Get something you can file paper in: a cardboard file, a three-ring-binder, an organizer folder with pockets, a clipboard… whatever works best for you.

It needs to be a file you can easily carry around with you, because that's what you are going to do in the next couple of weeks.

This is going to be your "Moving File".

Step # 5:

Print the *Moving Checklists* you downloaded and add them to your *Moving File*.

Step # 6:

Add every digital document you create or receive from others to your *Relocation Folder*. This includes 'Terms and Conditions' of your moving company, as well as quotes, attachments to emails, etc.

Documents you don't have to carry with you can stay digital, no need to print them.

But print each document you need to refer to often and quickly, and add it to your *Moving File*.

Step # 7:

Add every paper/printed document to your *Moving File*:

- *Moving Checklists* (printed)
- Quotes and letters from your moving company
- List of people you want to send a change-of-address note (download and print the *Change of Address – House Moving Checklist* and quickly jot down people or organizations when they pop up in your mind)
- Receipts (collect all receipts for moving-related expenses: for possible tax deduction, or reimbursement by employer)

- Your inventory (while 'work in progress'; and once finished)
- List of boxes with content

and so on.

Step # 8:

Create a place in your home where you keep important documents you want to keep handy but mustn't carry around with you. For instance:

- Passport of each family member
- Passport pictures of family members
- Pet's passport
- School records
- Car registration documentation
- Marriage license
- Birth certificates
- Will
- Legal documents
- Airline tickets

Add these to your *Trip Kit* or *Valuables* boxes (see next chapter).

Steps # 6, 7 and 8 are, of course, most important: Don't forget to file your records in the right folders, and you will never have to search for an important document!

3

Six Special Boxes
You Need

During your relocation you will come to a point when you'll need certain items: packing tape on your moving day; passports and kids' favorite toys during your trip; toothbrush and bedding on your first evening in the new home…

To avoid having to go on a wild-goose chase through your belongings, including opening a number of boxes to retrieve these items (or not being able to get them at all because the boxes are in your moving van or container), it will be best to collect what you'll need before hand.

Prepare the following boxes:

1. Moving File

Keep the *Moving File* with you and separated from the moving boxes at all times. Otherwise you run the risk of someone accidentally packing it into the moving van or container.

2. Moving Day Box

Add items like drinks and snacks for you, your helpers and movers. Plus packing tape, scissors, markers, tools, first aid kit, etc.

Label the box DO NOT MOVE – *MOVING DAY BOX* and keep it apart from the other moving boxes.

3. Trip Kit

These are the items you and your family will need while travelling. Add passports, prescription medicine, and so on (see Chapter 3).

Plus drinks and snacks, children's favorite toys and maybe a pillow, entertainment devices like iPad, mobile phone charger, sunglasses, dog's lead and bowl, and so on.

Label the box DO NOT MOVE – *TRIP KIT* and keep it separated from the other moving boxes.

4. Survival Box

Into this box you will pack what you'll need on your first day and/or evening in your new home: prescription medicine, toiletries, towels, bedding, flashlight, toilet paper, pet food, children's school needs, tea/coffee and UHT milk, electronic devices chargers, etc.

If you are moving abroad this box will need to contain everything you might require in the first couple of weeks in your new host city, before the container arrival. So these will most probably be a few boxes, and they'll need to travel as surplus baggage by air.

Label the box DO NOT MOVE – *SURVIVAL BOX* and keep it apart from the other moving boxes.

5. Valuables

Arrange how you will transport these–do not pack them with your other belongings. Keep them apart from your household goods, in a safe place (with neighbors or friends; locked in your car; etc.).

6. Important information about your home

Collect instruction manuals and other important information about your home for the people who will move in once you've left.

Label the box DO NOT MOVE – HOME INFORMATION and keep it separated from the other moving boxes.

4

Working with Your Checklists

In this book you'll find two Appendixes with all your *Moving Checklists*. While you're busy reading the top tips about moving I encourage you to add notes to your lists. There is also space for you to add your own special tasks.

Better yet, you can print these lists from these webpages:

*** www.tinyUrl.com/IntMovi

*** www.tinyUrl.com/MoviDom

Organize your diary

Make a note in your diary / calendar when to start with a new list (1 month before moving day / 3 weeks before moving day / etc.).

Always 2 lists

I recommend you always keep at least two *Moving Checklists* with you:

*1: the one you are currently working on

*2: the list you are going to use next

Task accomplished!

Also, I encourage you to tick the box off once you accomplished a task. Not only will you know you won't need to worry about this specific item any more, but the action of ticking off will give you a great feeling of satisfaction. Each tick is a small victory!

Personally I also love to scribble over list items I finished so my eyes can completely ignore what was written there and are only drawn to the tasks that are still to be completed. Gives me real satisfaction, too.

Now that you are set up perfectly for a smooth relocation let's have a look at a couple of challenges around house moving. And the top tips on how to overcome them:

5

I'm Singing
the *Moving Blues...*

As mentioned in the introduction, moving home is considered one of the most stressful events in life. It is sitting right on life's awful 'bottom ten list' of the most traumatic events with the likes of: death of a loved one, divorce, speaking in public, and so on. No wonder that before a relocation, so many people feel like the proverbial mouse sitting in front of a cobra, unable to process a thought or to move…

Thinking of what has to be done until we're happily settled in our new home can leave us overwhelmed, stressed and frustrated.

What I find helpful to get over the negative thinking are three things:

(*1) First, focus on the nice aspects of your relocation.

There is a new country, city or neighborhood waiting for you to be explored. Most probably you will also have a new job with a bright future. You will meet new people, have inspiring conversations and make new friends.

Plus you will be able to make a fresh start.

Isn't this exciting?

(*2) Second, concentrate on the next task only.

Yes, moving is a lot of work. But you don't have to do *everything* in one go! Relocation is a job done piece by piece, bit-by-bit. Forget about what you'll have to do later, only think of the next three tasks or so on your checklist–and then do them.

It's a bit like climbing a mountain: keep your eyes on the path and watch yourself take the next step, and then the next. Only occasionally look up and you will be amazed by the progress you managed to make!

(*3) Take a break

To cut some of the inevitable stress, make sure you do something to release it: take a couple of hours off from time to time. Get away from the moving boxes: Go to a movie. Exercise. Have a coffee at a coffee shop and read a book.

Whatever relaxes you and brings you joy: make time for it. You need these breaks to stay healthy–and sane!

6

Moving with Children

The most important advice if you are moving with children, in my opinion, is: Don't overthink it.

And number two: Don't dramatize your relocation.

From what I can see with friends who regularly move internationally, it seems most children are quite resilient. As long as you give them attention and a loving place they will be sad when you are leaving your home, but also excited once they arrive at the new place.

Moving day

For your moving days, I recommend you make a plan to keep your children safe and–let's call a spade a spade here–out of your hair.

For young children the best solution is to have somebody babysit them. Preferably *not* in the house you are packing up. Or moving into.

Older children may want to be involved. They can help you: There is plenty of work to do, right? But I would also make sure they can visit a friend for a play date at his house after an hour or two, to escape the chaos and bustle at your home.

Mementos

Ever since the birth of our children, our home seems to be filling up with 'things': toys, sports and music equipment, school books...

In our kids' primary school workbooks I find the funniest "What I did on my weekend" compositions, precious drawings and pictures. We are not planning to spend the rest of our life hauling our kids' first-grade schoolbooks around the globe with us, but we still want to keep these mementos. So what I do is scan these pages and save them as a computer file.

With their drawings and school or sports awards I do exactly the same.

Ditto with their letters to Santa Claus and the Easter Bunny.

Most art projects can't be scanned easily. But I can take a picture of them–and afterwards bin them without a bad conscience because the photos will always remain with us.

To be on the safe side, you should back up these files on an external hard drive or in the cloud–something I have to remind myself of only too often, too.

7

Requirements of the New School

In the town you're moving to, your child will obviously have to go to a new school.

Research your new host city's educational institutes as early as possible so you can secure a space for your child at the school of your choice.

Required documents

Usually, the new school will ask for a couple of documents that detail your child's progress, health, etc.

You can get in touch with the new school and inquire what their requirements are, then ask your present school for the necessary credentials.

Here are a few documents you might have to prepare for the new school:

- A list of every school attended including dates, contact names and addresses;
- Original report cards (with school seals);
- Copies of report cards and, if applicable, translations;
- Results of standardized tests and exams, in particular for English, Maths and Science;
- A list of current course outlines, so that the new school can assess what level your child is at;
- Letters from principals or teachers;

- A copy of your child's immunization records and most recent medical records.

Credentials

Some private schools out there strive to accept the best students only. I would therefore recommend you try to get the best possible school report for your child. Especially the assessment of preschoolers is highly subjective–and there is nothing wrong with nudging the school into the right direction. The better the school report and any other credentials, the more options you will have!

Extra-curricular activities

It may also be a good idea to keep records about your child's extra-curricular activities. You could make a list of all the extra hobbies and activities your child participates in outside of school, for instance:

- sports
- cultural activities
- clubs
- social and community activities
- volunteering
- jobs like baby-sitting, golf caddying, etc.

How about providing some extra details about these activities?

If your child is in the football team make a little file including a letter from the coach and a few pictures of the team.

For piano players, list the last couple of music pieces played plus the recitals your child took part of.

A member of a photography club may prepare a little portfolio of her/his work.

If your child worked as a caddy on the golf course it may be a good idea to ask the caddy master for a letter of reference.

As most schools welcome active and well-rounded children, this will show your daughter or son in the best light.

Plus it is a great way to celebrate your child's achievements. Therefore I would keep adding to these files as your child grows.

8

Choosing
Your Moving Company

On your *2 months to go - House Moving Checklist* you will come across the bullet point "Decide what services you need from your moving company". One of the possible options is to only rent a truck and ask your friends for help.

If you decide to commission the services of a moving company, however, you'll find a couple of helpful hints here:

To sort out the scammers from the reputable and experienced companies:

    a) Ask for a written cost estimate
    b) Ask for a copy of the contract: what is included? Insurance? Read it carefully.
    c) Lack of a website; very low price estimation; promise of the job done in an unusual short period of time; large deposits of money; demands of cash only payments: this looks like scam. Beware.

A detailed validation and binding cost estimation can be based on two things:

    I.   A representative of the moving company visits your home.
    II. Show them everything the movers will have to pack and move, or else you will face additional costs.
    III. You provide an inventory list.

IV. Make sure you list all of your belongings; for every additional item that is not on the list you will encounter additional costs.

Top Tip:

Before you ask for a detailed and binding price estimate by your moving company, and before you start working on your inventory list, make sure you purge your belongings (see Chapter 11).

Costs

Do you want to keep the relocation costs down as much as possible? Move:

**mid-month:

This is far less busy than the end of the month, and therefore fees are generally lower.

**mid-week:

Less busy than the weekend, and moving companies should give you a discount for this (AND you have the added plus that services like town offices, utilities, banks, etc. are open on your moving day–just in case you'll need their assistance).

Insurance

Moving companies generally offer a basic limited liability, free of charge.

But unfortunately this is no real insurance. I would recommend you make sure you have additional insurance coverage.

How? You have 2 options:

Option 1: Consult your insurance agent:

It could be that your current insurance covers your household goods while they are in transit–some homeowner's insurance policies do, for instance.

Option 2: Buy additional insurance from your moving company

Most moving companies offer this as an additional service for a fee.

9

Things Your Moving Company Will Not Move

Moving companies will say "no" to moving certain items because of legal, ethical or safety reasons.

Ask your moving company for their list of items they won't pack and/or move.

Generally, these things can be divided into **5 categories**:

Category #1: Pets

Animals can't be shipped inside a moving truck. Take your pet with you in your car or on the plane.

Category #2: Plants

Plants may perish in a moving vehicle. Short distances can be fine, longer ones aren't, especially if you are moving abroad with cargo container.

If there is a chance your plants will die on the move consider selling, giving them to friends or family or donating them to a local school or hospital.

Category #3: Irreplaceable belongings

Some of your household goods can't be replaced. These can be, amongst others:

    a. Things that are of sentimental value to you (photos, inherited items, etc.)
    b. Cash, or other financial means like (paper) bonds

c. Collections (stamps, coins, etc.) or collectors' items

d. Items of high value like jewelry or electronics

Moving companies don't like to be responsible for such items–read the fine print in your contract.

I recommend you keep these items in a safe place and then transport them together with your *Valuables*.

Category #4: Explosive, corrosive or flammable items

Law forbids transporting any hazardous items. This category includes:

- Fireworks
- Weapons and ammunition
- Car batteries
- Gasoline and motor oil (lawn mower; chain saw; etc.)
- Pesticides, fertilizers, weed killers
- Pool chemicals
- Paint and paint thinners
- Charcoal
- Propane gas tanks (for barbeques)
- Fire extinguishers
- Lighters and matches
- Cleaning supplies / bleach
- Aerosol cans (deodorant, hair spray)
- Acids / Ammonia
- Alcohol / Liquor

Category #5: Food

Except for canned/tinned food or items with a long shelve life. Non-perishable food in sealed containers is ok, even for international relocations.

If you are moving a short distance only you are free to transport whatever food with you in your car.

Leave anything like this behind!

Don't try to 'smuggle' such things into your moving boxes. Neither your moving nor your insurance company will cover any loss or damage to your belongings if there is an accident because of 'forbidden' items.

Best to give these items away or discard of them in an environmentally safe way.

10

Sort Out Your Home: Why

As mentioned before, you should get rid of everything you don't need anymore, as well as the items the moving company will refuse to move, before you start packing your moving boxes, and preferably even before you get a binding estimate by your moving company.

Sorting out your household goods will help you to:

*a) Save time:

Packing something you won't need anymore, and then unpacking and stowing it away in your new home? What a waste of time.

*b) Save money:

Moving companies' charges are based on how much you own: The less they have to move the cheaper it will be for you! So basically each box you pack has a price tag attached to it...

*c) *Make* money:

You may not use an item anymore, but this doesn't mean it is useless–or worthless! Sell your pre-loved items and earn money (see below for more tips on how to do this).

Not only children, but also we adults are not keen to tidy up. Am I right or am I right?

As far as I'm concerned, I tend to keep 'stuff' in our garage or attics, thinking its presence there doesn't hurt anybody.

An upcoming relocation is the perfect time to go through this 'stuff' and decide whether it is *really* worth the effort, time and money to take it with you. The more items you move the more boxes you need, the bigger the moving van needs to be, the more packing, carrying, unpacking there will be for you...

Consider:

Import restrictions

The first thing to do for you: find out if your new host country, state or province has any import restrictions. These may include firearms, alcohol, DVDs, books, even pets...

Get the list of 'forbidden' things. Or else you'll loose your belongings, and find yourself with a fine, or even worse.

International relocation: Take everything, or leave everything?

If you are facing an international relocation, ask yourself a question of principle before you start going through your household goods:

Will it be better for you to pack everything you own and ship it? Or would it be better to sell everything and start afresh overseas?

If you're transferred abroad by your employer or have signed a contract with a new company, find out what their conditions are for moving employees' households. They will most certainly pay for some of your removal costs.

A few advantages of selling everything:

- Save the cost of packing and shipping your household goods across the seven seas;
- Save the cost of insurance for your belongings while they're in transfer;

- Save the cost for temporary furnished accommodation while you wait for your container (several weeks if not months);
- You might not be able to use many of your electrical devices, appliances and electronics–if your new host country has a different voltage from the place you're currently living in. You may have to buy new ones in your new host city;
- The climate in your host city may damage your furniture or pictures (air too humid in tropics, too dry in desert climates);
- Storage? In my opinion this is only a good idea if you're away for a short period of time (6 months to a year). In the long run, it can be expensive and risky (water, earthquakes, insects, etc. can damage your belongings). Plus: will you really want these items a couple of years down the line? Maybe better sell them now, unless they have emotional value for you;
- Buying second-hand furniture, electrical devices, appliances, etc. from expats who are leaving the country is fairly easy in many places;
- In some places it is also easy to rent furnished homes;
- If you decide to sell your household goods you should keep what is 'essential' (heirlooms, things with emotional value, etc.). Pack these into two or three boxes and take them with you as air fright.

In conclusion: Selling your belongings and starting afresh may save you time and money. Although it seems scary at first, it is a sensible and economical option for many people.

Some advantages of shipping all of your belongings:

- Your own furniture and household goods will help you feel at home in a foreign place;
- If you have good quality furniture it is most probably more economical to ship them abroad than selling them and buying new ones;

- Trying to sell a large amount of furniture and household goods takes a huge amount of time–much more than packing them.

In conclusion: Having your own belongings abroad will help you with settling in. It is more economical for many people.

Most expatriates take their household goods with them wherever they go.

Top Tip:

#1 - If you choose this option, check out if your new host country applies import restrictions, and find out their voltage (see Chapter 14). You might not be able to take all of your belongings.

#2 - Carefully sorting through your household will be necessary and important–follow the tips in the next few paragraphs as well as Chapter 12.

How big is your new home?

Draw a floor plan of your new home and decide where you will place your furniture. Is there enough space for each piece of furniture you own? Or will you have to sell something?

Think of the storage in your new home, e.g. garage, attics, basement: How much space is there? How many boxes of 'stuff' you don't use right now but think you might need sometimes in the future can be stored?

Will you have a garden or yard? If not, it might be better to get rid of your gardening tools, lawn mower, etc.

11

Sort Out Your Home: How

Get motivated for action

As mentioned before, you will spend effort, muscle power, time and money on each item you'll pack and move to your new home. Do you want to do this for something you haven't used in ages? Or something that is broken and not worth having fixed?

See, the purging *is* necessary.

If you can, ask a good friend to help you–she or he will be more 'objective' in judging the value of an item.

*Play some good music.

*Slip into comfortable clothes.

*And let's start!

Prepare boxes plus black rubbish bags

What you will need:

- 1 box marked 'sell'
- 1 box marked 'give away'
- 1 box unmarked (plus a few spare ones)
- 1 black trash bag (plus a few spare ones)
- a felt marker, paper and pen

Sort your belongings into 4 categories:

*Category #1: Keep

Three sorts of items can stay with you:

1. Things you need and use

2. Things you love

3. Things that will find a place in your new home

Everything else will have to go.

Remind yourself: You don't owe anything to anybody! These items live in *your* home. As much as you are entitled to deny other people to enter your home you are entitled to allow 'stuff' into your home–or not.

Moving home is *the* opportunity to get rid of unwanted gifts, for instance. Tell aunt Sarah that unfortunately, her vase didn't survive the removal... No lie, is it? (Just find a tactful way to let your aunt know that she needn't bother presenting you with a replacement.)

Try to be ruthless: it's fun! And liberating.

*Category #2: Sell

Everything that is useful and in good shape can be sold.

You will, however, have to decide how much time you want to spend on selling.

For a garage sale, you will have to go through your items, mark them with a price tag and arrange them on the day of the sale.

If you are selling on eBay, Craig's List or Gumtree, you will have to take a picture, upload it and write a description of the item.

*Category #3: Give away

Things you can't or don't want to sell can be donated to charity.

Plants may find a new home in a hospital, old age home or school.

Ditto for books you won't read again.

*Category #4: Trash

What is broken and useless should go into the trash bags.

Get started with the sorting

Work a room

Go through your household goods room by room.

Stand in the door of the room, then turn left and work your way through the room clockwise.

Look at–or even better: touch–every item you see and decide *quickly*:

- Stay or go?
- Sell or give away?
- Trash?

Trash lands in the black bins immediately.

'Give away' items go into the box designated for things you give to others.

Put things you are planning to *sell* into the box marked 'sell'.

If you decide to *keep* an item you can either leave it where it is so it will get packed later by you or the packers.

Or you can pack it into one of the empty, unmarked boxes you prepared for this occasion. In this case, I recommend you write down the content of the box and once it is full, and mark it clearly with your felt marker.

Work the next room

And so on, sort through the household goods in your entire home, including garage, shed, attics, etc.

Finishing your purging session

Done?

*- Get rid of the 'trash'.

*- Put the 'give away' boxes into the trunk of your car.

Take them to your next local charity. OR:

Call the charity to make arrangements for them to come and collect the boxes.

*- Box marked 'sell': decide on how you want to sell these items (see next Chapter).

12

Selling Your ‚Stuff':
Three Options

Option 1: Garage sale

This is probably the easiest way to sell your unwanted items: arrange them in your garage, mark each item with a price tag, and write a list of items and prices (in case a price tag comes off, and to protect yourself against cheaters).

Then advertise the date and time of your sale in local supermarkets, schools, etc.

On the day of your sale, open your garage door and start selling.

Top Tips:

#1 - Ask neighbors if they are interested in selling some of their belongings, too: you might be able to organize a "neighborhood super sale".

#2 - Plan your garage sale for a Sunday: people will be relaxed and have time to browse.

#3 - Make sure you have enough change.

Option 2: Online selling platforms (for instance eBay)

You can sell your unwanted items on an Internet platform like eBay (www.ebay.com), Gumtree (check on Wikipedia if Gumtree is present in your country) or Craigslist (find the different national and local websites listed on: www.craigslist.org/about/sites).

Check out the sellers' information for details on how it works. Here is a very basic overview of the process:

1) Register

2) List your item with a description and a photo

3) Get paid

4) Ship the item to the buyer

Top Tips:

#1 - Take beautiful pictures of your items. They'll help to sell them.

#2 - When deciding on a price for your item, take the shipping costs into account. You will have to post the item you sell.

Option 3: Auction

For your larger belongings, you might want to consider an auction.

Auctioneers will collect your items, charging a fee for this.

Upon the sale you will receive a percentage of the sales price.

13

International Relocation: How Does This Work?

In the past chapters I mentioned the option of moving abroad a couple of times. Those of you who are not embarking on an international relocation, you can skip this entire chapter.

Those of you who *are* about to move abroad may be wondering about some of the differences between moving within the same country and a relocation overseas, and you may ask: How does an international relocation actually work?

Here are a few pointers

How do you transfer your household goods from here to there?

There are three ways: by road, sea or air.

** Road transport

This is the method of choice wherever it is possible. If you are moving from England to Spain, for instance, you will want to transport your items in a moving van.

Your household goods don't have to be secured in any special ways (see below) if you travel by road, except for wrapping them in miles of bubble wrap.

** Sea transport

Between continents, road transport becomes too expensive or even hazardous. For many expats who are moving to a country far away, sea transport is the method of choice. It has relatively low costs but is slow (a couple of weeks between continents).

For this mode of transport, your belongings need extra packing for safety. A bookshelf or a piano will be secured in a wooden crate; bulky items as well as smaller, fragile household goods will be generously wrapped in bubble wrap.

Everything will finally be packed into a metal cargo container.

As there is limited space in the container you have to make sure your household goods fit into it. If you need additional space, or if your belongings will only fill half a container, consider *Groupage*: that's when a container is filled with items from two or several owners. Each of them pays a share of the transport costs. Talk to your moving company if you are interested in *Groupage*.

** Air transport

Obviously the quickest mode of transport. As it is very expensive, many expats choose to only bring the most important things with them, the ones they need in the first few days after arrival (your *Survival Boxes*).

Facing the removal costs, some people choose to sell all of their belongings and start their household afresh in the new country (see Chapter 10). In this case, the couple of 'essential' belongings like photo books, etc. can be transported by airfreight.

Pets who relocate internationally will usually travel by air.

Airlines have clear instructions about how items have to be packed and secured so they can be transported in a plane.

** A combination of different transport modes

If the distance between the old and the new home is not too big, expats may use only road transport.

But most people who move abroad use a combination of the different modes of transport. Household goods are usually ferried by road or sea transport, whereas the family members and pets travel by air.

Professional moving company

Because the packing and international transport is complicated you will have to use the services of a professional moving company.

Customs clearance

Once your household goods arrive in the new country, they will have to be cleared by the local customs authorities. International moving companies will fill out the forms for you and make sure your belongings are cleared as soon as possible. Nevertheless, this process can take a couple of days or even weeks.

Electrical devices, appliances and electronics

Before you pack for an international relocation google the voltage in the country you are moving to: Some countries use 110/120 volts, others 220/230 volts.

If you try to use your US hairdryer in Europe all you will achieve is a fried device.

Wikipedia has a list of the voltage and frequency used in each country:
www.en.wikipedia.org/wiki/Mains_electricity_by_country

Electronics like computers, digital cameras, DVD players, etc. may allow a range of voltages and hertz systems, I understand. Please do your own, thorough research, though.

** What to do if there are differences in voltage

There are so-called step-down transformers if your devices work on a different voltage from the country you are moving to. However, I hear they are not completely reliable (please do your own research).

If you are faced with this situation, selling your vacuum cleaner, toaster, etc. before moving and then buying new electrical devices and appliances when you arrive in your new host city may be an economical option (especially second-hand from other expats who are moving away).

**Same voltage, but different plugs and power outlets

If there is 'only' a difference between power plug points/plugs, you have two options:

Adapters: Use an adapter between the foreign plug and the power outlet.

Change the plug: You can cut off your device's plug and attach a plug from the country you are moving to. It's easier than it sounds–even I can do it. It may be the best option for an item you use often like a toaster or a vacuum cleaner.

Cars

Should you ship your car abroad?

** The short answer is:
No.

** The long answer is:
You can do it *if*:

- it is permitted (cars with the steering wheel on the left side cannot be permanently used in a country that has left-handed traffic, for instance);
- you did the math and it is more cost effective to take your car abroad than to buy a new one in your host country (include taxes, custom duties, etc. in your

calculations, as well as aspects like marine insurance, if applicable);
- you will be able to comfortably use your car in your host country (in some countries small cars are generally driven, in other big ones, and there are good reasons for this: cruising through and parking a minivan in one of the medieval cities in Italy will be a challenge, for instance);
- your car is very precious to you and/or not a common model (e.g. vintage cars);
- you have a lot of time and patience (lots of procedures to be mastered and forms to be filled out…).

The same thoughts apply more or less for other motor vehicles.

14

Moving Your Pet Abroad

The good news is:

Compared to you, your pet will move with only a very limited amount of belongings.

The bad news is:

The process of moving your pet from one country to another can be complicated, tedious and expensive.

Start early!

Many countries apply firm restrictions to pet immigration.

Special vaccinations are often required; these have to be administered a couple of months before travelling, as often the antibodies have to be verified through a blood test a month or so before travelling.

Almost every country requires pets to be equipped with a microchip before immigration. Plus the paper work has to be up-to-date and correct.

Some countries insist on quarantines–Australia requires 7 months of quarantine for dogs!

In some instances your pet may not even be allowed to immigrate with you and you may have to find a new home for it.

Also, if your pet has to travel by plane you should book the flight as soon as possible to make sure there is space for your animal.

Do thorough research!

Countries have different requirements. Find out what your host country's rules and regulations are and follow them to the dot. Or else your pet's immigration will be denied and you'll have to wave goodbye to it.

5 Steps for moving your pet internationally:

Step #1: Contact your host country's consulate

As I just mentioned, do this as early as possible.

Ask about:

- Which pets can–and can't–immigrate
- Restrictions for importing pets into the country
- Breed or age restrictions
- Quarantine; if yes, for how long
- Which vaccinations are required
- Which tests are required
- Micro chipping
- Which documents are required at arrival/immigration
- Will there be any import fees
- Do pets have to clear customs
- How long will it take to clear customs

Step #2: Contact your airline

Ask how your pet will be carried: in the cabin (e.g. cats or small dogs) or as special baggage, which means they will be in a ventilated and heated hold in the plane's 'belly'. To avoid stress for your pet, it will be semi-dark and quiet there.

A few things to ask:

- What size of carrier box will my pet have to travel in?

- How long before the flight has my pet to be at the airport?
- Where do I check it in?
- Which documents do I need for the check in?
- Which documents do I bring when picking my pet up upon arrival?
- Does my pet need customs clearance?
- Where do I pick it up?
- What is the cost of the air transport?

Step #3: Contact your pet's vet

Once you know your new host country's pet immigration rules and regulations as well as the airline's, I recommend you meet your vet and discuss the following:

*a) Vaccination schedule:

Which vaccinations are required, which recommended; when to administer them; blood tests, if needed; a check-up needed before travelling; etc.

*b) Microchip: update your contact details

*c) Your pet's health records: get a copy of them

*d) Your pet's comfort while on the move:

Is your pet healthy enough for travelling? Ask about: best way to travel; carrier box; sedatives; food and water; where to quarantine, if applicable; etc.

*e) Any recommendations for your pet's life in the new host country

Step #4: Book your pet's transport

As soon as your vet has answered your questions you should arrange for your pet's transport.

While travelling by car, train, ship, etc. is not too complicated to figure out, there are a few things to consider when moving your pet by air:

On a plane there are only two places where your pet can travel safely and comfortably: in the cabin or *in the hold*. The latter may even be less stressful for your animal as it is darkened and quiet.

The baggage/cargo area of a plane is usually not heated and your pet could suffer, even die, depending on the circumstances.

Step #5: Make your pet ready for travelling

Buy your pet a collar, if it hasn't one yet, and attach 2 identification tags to them:

One tag with your current contact information, and the other tag with your new contact information.

Should somebody other than you collect your pet at the airport make sure he or she has a picture of your animal.

It is also a good idea to attach a photo of your pet to its carrier box, and to carry one with you when you're travelling. Just to be on the safe side.

Relocation services for pets

You can find service providers who assist you with moving your pet. It can make things much easier.

Pick a reputable company.

Their fees seem to be quite hefty–that's why one of my expat friends calls her well-travelled pet "the million dollar dog".

15

Moving Your Pet
Within the Same Country

This is a lot easier than an international relocation with your pet!

Some of the points mentioned in the previous chapter are applicable here too, though:

Appointment with the vet

*a) Make sure your pet's vaccinations are up-to-date.

*b) Ask for a copy of your pet's health records.

*c) Discuss your pet's comfort while on the move:

Is your pet healthy enough for travelling? Ask about: best way to travel; carrier box; sedatives; food and water; etc.

*d) Microchip: I recommend you have your pet micro chipped. Even if your cat is as lazy as ours, who sleeps 22 hours a day and never leaves our property (going for a little stroll in the garden is the most exertion she finds appropriate), she might be confused in your new home and maybe get lost in the neighborhood. With a microchip, anybody who finds her can contact you.

Travelling by car:

Stop often so your pet can stretch its legs.

Bring enough water and food.

Never leave your pet in a closed vehicle; it can get too hot, which promptly leads to death.

Travelling by air:

Please refer to the previous chapter where you will find the top tips about this way of travelling for your pet.

Identification for your pet

Finding themselves in a strange new place, many pets become nervous, run away and become lost.

Buy your pet a collar, if it hasn't one yet, and attach an identification tag to it with your contact details. Just in case–this may help finding your furry friend quicker if need be.

16

Conclusion:
Your Action Plan

Congratulations! You made it through the book and have hopefully profited from the many tips and tricks for the preparation of your relocation.

If you haven't already done so, it is now time to put everything into action. Here is a quick action plan:

Step #1: Download your *Moving Checklists*

You'll find these lists in the two Appendixes later in this book. Yet I recommend you download them in pdf format so you can carry them around with you, add notes and tick off what you accomplished.

Here is the link to the International Moving Checklists collection:

www.tinyUrl.com/IntMovi

This link will take you to the Domestic Moving Checklists collection:

www.tinyUrl.com/MoviDom

Step #2: Save these lists to your Relocation Folder

Step #3: Print your Moving Checklists (Chapter 3)

Keep them in your *Moving File*

Step #4: Create your six special boxes (Chapter 4)

Moving File, Moving Day Box, Trip Kit, Survival Box, Valuables, Important information about your home

If you don't add the items right now because you still need them, keep a list of what you will add to the boxes at a later stage.

Step #5: Time to start with a new list (Chapter 5)

Note in your diary when it is time to start working on the next *Moving Checklist*: 1 month before moving day, 3 weeks before moving day, and so on.

Step #6: Do the tasks that are listed on your Moving Checklists (Chapter 5)

Step #7: Tick off what you accomplished

I wish you the best of luck with the preparation of your relocation!

Barbara Bruhwiler

PS: I would love to hear from you! Say "hi", send me your questions, and, of course, let me know it if you liked this book. Simply write to: Autorin.B@gmail.com

Thank You

Many thanks, dear reader!

I hope you like this book and find it useful.

Can I please ask you for a small favor?

Other readers rely on your feedback. If you believe this book is worth sharing, could you please take a few seconds to rate it?

This link will take you directly to the book's page in your preferred book store:

www.tinyUrl.com/houseMovi

Your feedback will help other readers, and for this they will be grateful. And so will I.

Thank you very much!

More Books
by Barbara

Barbara Bruhwiler is a bestselling author in Germany.

She wrote a series of Business & Career books
– in German – that all climbed the Bestseller List.

You can find them here:

www.tinyUrl.com/booksBBr

Appendix 1:

Checklists for your

Domestic Relocation

Domestic Relocation:
Checklist 1
2 Months before Moving

ORGANIZE YOUR PAPERWORK
- ☐ Open a new folder called Relocation Folder on your computer
- ☐ Create your (paper) Moving File
- ☐ _____
- ☐ _____

YOUR PET
- ☐ Research if there are any special requirements in the state / province you're relocating to
- ☐ Contact the airline and ask your questions (if applicable)
- ☐ Arrange the necessary vaccinations
- ☐ Arrange for your pet to be micro chipped
- ☐ Ask for a pet's passport
- ☐ Get a copy of your pet's veterinarian file
- ☐ Ask vet for tips on moving your pet
- ☐ Arrange air transport (if applicable)
- ☐ _____
- ☐ _____

CHOOSING AND DEALING WITH YOUR MOVING COMPANY

☐ Decide whether you're moving your household goods – or bring nothing to your new host city and purchase everything there

☐ Decide what services you need from your moving company:

a) truck rental

b) hiring movers for transport only

c) transport and packing of a part of your belongings by movers

d) transport and packing of all of your belongings by movers

e) transport, packing and additional services by movers

☐ Contact your employer; see if they are paying for your relocation

☐ If your employer is paying for your move, read their moving policy to find out what services you are entitled to

☐ Decide on your budget

☐ Decide what date you want to move (mid-week / mid month = less expensive and less busy)

☐ Add any important information like quotes and receipts to your *Moving File*

☐ Find contact details of moving companies:

a) Ask friends for a recommendation, OR

b) Google "moving company" + your area

☐ Research moving companies; look at previous customers' reviews

☐ Contact 3 moving companies to compare prices

☐ Ask them to inspect your home before they prepare a quote (if they need to pack; probably not needed if they only have to transport your belongings)

- ☐ Show the moving agent EVERYTHING that you need to be moved
- ☐ Mention if anything else, something that is not in your home, will be added
- ☐ Mention what they DON'T need to move because you are selling or giving it away
- ☐ Discuss the date you want to move
- ☐ Compare the quotes you get from the moving companies:
  a) price
  b) services offered
  c) conditions
  d) insurance offered
- ☐ Choose a moving company and sign the contract
- ☐ Keep the name, phone number and email address of your contact person with the moving company in your *Moving File* and save it in your mobile phone
- ☐ Inform the moving company about changes, for instance:
  a) additional items to be moved
  b) items that you gave away or stored
  c) change of moving date
- ☐ _____
- ☐ _____

Top Tip: If your friends help you moving, consider what you'll do in case somebody causes damage to one of your items or your home. Do your friends have insurance for such damages? Can you organize extra insurance for your moving day? Try not to let a damage ruin your friendship.

NOTICE
- ☐ Give notice at work
- ☐ Give notice to your landlord
- ☐ Give notice to your domestic or other employees
- ☐ Inform the school that you're moving away
- ☐ _____
- ☐ _____

HOME
- ☐ Get in contact with estate agent
- ☐ To recoup your bond: arrange for a property inspection
- ☐ Sell your house
- ☐ _____
- ☐ _____

PLACE YOU ARE MOVING TO
- ☐ Start researching the town/community you are moving to
- ☐ Apply to a new school
- ☐ Make travel arrangements
- ☐ Arrange interim accommodation at your destination
- ☐ _____
- ☐ _____

COLLECT IMPORTANT DOCUMENTS
- ☐ Birth Certificates
- ☐ Marriage Certificate
- ☐ Medical documentation
- ☐ Dental file
- ☐ Vaccination records

- ☐ Medical prescriptions
- ☐ Ask doctor, dentist, etc. for referrals in your new host city
- ☐ School records and other recommended documents
- ☐ Veterinarian file
- ☐ Copies of financial records
- ☐ Copies of legal records
- ☐ Insurance: call your agent and ask if you need to make any changes to your policy, or even have to get a new insurance policy
- ☐ _____
- ☐ _____

SORT OUT ITEMS YOU MIGHT NOT BE ABLE TO TAKE WITH YOU

- ☐ Organize permission to take unusual items to another state / province: guns, crocodile skin handbag (endangered species), etc.
- ☐ Sell or give away plants
- ☐ Get rid of explosive, corrosive or flammable items like fireworks, matches, cleaning fluids, acids, chemistry sets, aerosol cans, ammunition, paint and thinner, etc.
- ☐ Use up or discard poisons like weed-killer, fuel in your lawn mower, etc.
- ☐ Follow the instructions given by your moving company
- ☐ _____
- ☐ _____

MOVING YOUR CAR OR OTHER MOTOR VEHICLES

☐ Decide if you're taking or leaving your car or other motor vehicles

☐ If you want to take it, contact moving company

☐ Prepare documents

☐ Have your car serviced

☐ Follow instructions given by moving company

☐ _____

☐ _____

GO THROUGH YOUR BELONGINGS

☐ Create a floor plan of your new home and see if all your furniture fits in

☐ Note which items are too bulky for the new place

☐ Note which items will need special packing or extra insurance coverage

☐ _____

☐ _____

'SHRINK' YOUR HOUSEHOLD GOODS

☐ Eat the food in your fridge, freezer and pantry

☐ Finish the wine, beer and spirits you own

☐ Use up cosmetic supplies, cleaning agents and other household items

☐ Sort out your belongings (refer to book for tips)

☐ Organize storage facility

☐ Give items away to family and friends (house plants, books, etc.)

☐ Organize a garage sale

☐ Sell things via online auction service (e.g. eBay)

☐ Donate clothing, books, left over food, drinks, cleaning agents, etc. to charity

☐ _____

☐ _____

Top Tip: Ask the charity for receipts showing the items' approximate value – you might get a tax deduction

FINANCES

☐ Cancel automated payments (e.g. rent, post box, levy, club memberships,)

☐ Settle any outstanding bills

☐ _____

☐ _____

Domestic Relocation:
Checklist 2
1 Month before Moving

PREPARE THE FAMILY
- ☐ Make farewell visits to places with happy memories
- ☐ Organize a going-away party for your children
- ☐ Organize a going-away party for yourselves
- ☐ _____
- ☐ _____

IN AND AROUND YOUR HOME
- ☐ Return library books, DVDs, etc.
- ☐ Return borrowed, checked-out and rented items
- ☐ Get things back you have lent or rented out
- ☐ Make any home repairs you have committed to
- ☐ _____
- ☐ _____

UTILITIES, MAIL, ETC.
- ☐ Ask for utilities to be disconnected
  (refer to *Change of Address – Moving Checklist*)
- ☐ Ask Post Office to forward your mail to your new address
- ☐ Ask neighbor to look out for mail after you moved
- ☐ Organize utilities to be connected in your new host city
- ☐ _____

Tip Tips:
- Schedule **disconnection** of services for 3 days **after your moving day** (allow for cleaning).
- Schedule **connection** of services in new city for 2 days **before your arrival day** (allow for inspection and/or cleaning).

ORGANIZE PACKING MATERIAL
- ☐ Boxes
- ☐ Tape
- ☐ Bubble wrap
- ☐ Stuffing/padding
- ☐ Markers
- ☐ Dish barrels, if needed
- ☐ Wardrobe boxes, if needed
- ☐ _____
- ☐ _____

Top Tip: If you are using a moving company ask them to deliver the packing material now.

START PACKING
- ☐ Start with items that are not constantly in use
- ☐ Pack things you won't use in the next few weeks (like winter resp. summer clothes)
- ☐ Disassemble outdoor items like swing set, wendy house
- ☐ Take pictures of things you are about to disassemble
- ☐ Place all screws, bolts, brackets in small (Ziploc) plastic bags, and tape this to the disassembled item
- ☐ Start disassembling pre-fabricated furniture
- ☐ _____
- ☐ _____

PACKING BEST PRACTISE

- ☐ Label every box clearly (content, room to go)
- ☐ Write a number on the lid and the side of each box
- ☐ Use the number to prepare an inventory list of each box
- ☐ Note damages on furniture in your inventory list
- ☐ _____
- ☐ _____

WHITE GOODS ETC.

- ☐ Check moving instructions for washing machine etc.
- ☐ Organize a plumber to prepare it for transport
- ☐ Arrange for an expert to install fixtures upon your arrival in the new home, if needed
- ☐ _____
- ☐ _____

PETS, BULKY AND DIFFICULT ITEMS

- ☐ Arrange transport of pets
- ☐ Plan how to transport bulky items
- ☐ Plan how to transport difficult items like house plants
- ☐ _____
- ☐ _____

FINANCES

- ☐ Open bank accounts in your new host city
- ☐ Apply for Post Office box in your new host city
- ☐ Organize sufficient cash for the relocation
- ☐ Plan for tips for the movers
- ☐ Organize form of payment for moving company
- ☐ Pay deposit for moving company
- ☐ _____
- ☐ _____

CHANGE OF ADDRESS NOTIFICATIONS

- ☐ Organize inexpensive ways of staying in touch with family and friends
- ☐ Prepare emails for change of address notifications
- ☐ For addresses: see *Change of Address – Moving Checklist*
- ☐ Get 'change of address' notifications from post office for those without email address
- ☐ Prepare and send these
- ☐ _____
- ☐ _____

Top Tips:

- Organize inexpensive ways of staying in touch with friends and family, such as Skype, Viber, WhatsApp, Facetime, Google Chat, etc.
- Open accounts for yourself, and maybe also for your parents (who may not be so Internet savvy).
- Add the contact info to your 'change of address notifications'.

Domestic Relocation: Checklist 3

3 Weeks before Moving

ORGANIZE HELPERS

☐ Babysitter for your kids for moving day

☐ Somebody to look after your pet on moving day

☐ Friends etc. as helpers for moving day

☐ Babysitter and helpers for moving-in day at your new home (if not the same day as moving day)

☐ _____

☐ _____

DAY OFF

☐ Notify employer you need a day off for moving

☐ _____

☐ _____

SCHOOL RECORDS

☐ Ask for school records to be forwarded to new school

☐ _____

☐ _____

CLEANING OF NEW HOME

☐ Confirm that your new home will be thoroughly cleaned

☐ If not sure, arrange to have it cleaned by somebody other than you before you move in

☐ _____

☐ _____

HIDING PLACES

☐ Empty secret hiding places for valuables
☐ Collect hidden spare house keys
☐ _____
☐ _____

START PREPARING YOUR SPECIAL BOXES:

Moving Day Box

☐ List the items you will need on moving day
☐ For instance: drinks, snacks, packing tape, scissors, markers, first aid kit, etc.
☐ Start collecting items and putting into this box, if not constantly in use
☐ Label the box DO NOT MOVE – MOVING DAY BOX
☐ Keep this box separated from other moving boxes
☐ _____
☐ _____

Trip Kit

☐ List the items you and your family will need while travelling
☐ For instance: passports, visa, pet's travel documents, marriage certificates, school records, prescription medicine, etc. (see Chapter 3)

- ☐ Add drinks and snacks, children's favorite toys and maybe a pillow, entertainment devices like iPad, mobile phone charger, sunglasses, dog's lead and bowl, foreign currency, etc.
- ☐ Start collecting items and putting into this box, if not constantly in use
- ☐ Label the box DO NOT MOVE – TRIP KIT
- ☐ Keep separated from other moving boxes
- ☐ _____
- ☐ _____

Survival Box

- ☐ List the first things you will need in your new home
- ☐ For instance: prescription medicine for a few weeks, toiletries, towels, bedding, flashlight, toilet paper, pet food, children's school needs, tea/coffee and UHT milk, electronic devices chargers, etc.
- ☐ Start collecting items and putting into this box, if not constantly in use
- ☐ Label the box DO NOT MOVE – SURVIVAL BOX
- ☐ Keep separated from other moving boxes
- ☐ _____
- ☐ _____

Valuables

- ☐ List your precious belongings
- ☐ Take pictures
- ☐ Organize storage, if needed (bank safe etc.)
- ☐ Plan how you will move them
- ☐ Make arrangements for their transport
- ☐ Take extra insurance coverage for the transport, if needed

☐ Keep them in a safe place, for instance: with neighbors or friends; locked in your car

☐ _____

☐ _____

Important Information About Your Home – For The Next Tenant/Owner

☐ Collect instruction manuals

☐ Collect other important information about your home

☐ Put them into this box

☐ Add your (new) contact details

☐ Label the box:
DO NOT MOVE – HOME INFORMATION

☐ Keep separated from other moving boxes

☐ _____

☐ _____

SELF-PACKERS

☐ Start serious packing

☐ _____

☐ _____

PACKING BEST PRACTISE

☐ Label every box clearly (content, room to go)

☐ Write a number on the lid and the side of each box

☐ Use the number to prepare an inventory list of each box

☐ Note damages on furniture in your inventory list

☐ _____

☐ _____

DISASSEMBLING BEST PRACTISE

- ☐ Take pictures of things you are about to disassemble
- ☐ Place all screws, bolts, brackets in small (Ziploc) plastic bags, and tape this to the disassembled item
- ☐ _____
- ☐ _____

FIXING

- ☐ Remove any fixtures you are taking with you
- ☐ Fix damages to the apartment / house
- ☐ _____
- ☐ _____

Domestic Relocation:
Checklist 4

1 Week before Moving

PAPERWORK

- ☐ Re-check that all paperwork for old and new place is complete
- ☐ _____
- ☐ _____

TRAVEL ARRANGEMENTS

- ☐ Re-confirm travel arrangements for family
- ☐ Re-confirm travel arrangements for pets
- ☐ _____
- ☐ _____

PETS:

- ☐ Buy your pet a collar
- ☐ Attach 2 identification tags to your pet's collar
- ☐ Write old contact details on one identification tag
- ☐ Write new contact details on the other identification tag
- ☐ _____
- ☐ _____

IN/AROUND YOUR HOME

☐ Plan how you will spend your last night in your old home

☐ Mow the lawn for the last time

☐ Clean the lawn mower and empty petrol and oil

☐ Empty garden hose

☐ Empty your locker at gym or club

☐ Collect dry cleaning

☐ _____

☐ _____

FOOD AND DRINKS

☐ Plan meals for the last days

☐ Completely finish the food in your freezer and pantry

☐ Organize food and drinks for moving day – including helper and packers

☐ _____

☐ _____

SUITCASES

☐ Pack a suitcase for each family member

☐ Add enough clothes to wear for a few days

☐ Add personal items

☐ _____

☐ _____

KEEP THESE SEPARATED FROM YOUR OTHER MOVING BOXES:

☐ *Moving Day Box*

☐ *Trip Kit*

- ☐ *Survival Box*
- ☐ *Valuables*
- ☐ *Important information about your home*

Top Tip: Keep these boxes, as well as the suitcases, in a (empty) bathroom. Stick a note onto the bathroom door: DO NOT TAKE ANY BOXES IN HERE.

Close the door on moving day.

- ☐ _____
- ☐ _____

SELF-PACKERS

- ☐ Keep packing
- ☐ Clean shelves, cupboards, etc. when they are empty
- ☐ _____
- ☐ _____

ELECTRONICS

- ☐ Back up your computer hard drive
- ☐ Secure back-up (Cloud? *Valuables* box?); don't pack it into same box as computer
- ☐ Take photos of cables
- ☐ Unplug electronics at least 24 hours before packing
- ☐ Disassemble and carefully pack
- ☐ Add remote controls
- ☐ _____
- ☐ _____

VALUABLES

- ☐ Empty your safe deposit box
- ☐ Secure these items for safe travel
- ☐ _____

PLAN OF NEW HOME

☐ Draw a plan of your new home

☐ Draw furniture on it, so your helpers or moving company knows where to place them

☐ _____

☐ _____

Domestic Relocation:
Checklist 5

Change of Address List

WHO NEEDS TO KNOW
ABOUT YOUR RELOCATION

PROFESSIONAL SERVICES
- ☐ Doctors
- ☐ Dentists
- ☐ Insurance agent
- ☐ Lawyer
- ☐ Accountant
- ☐ Bank
- ☐ Broker
- ☐ Credit Card company
- ☐ Auto Finance company
- ☐ Veterinarian
- ☐ _____
- ☐ _____

Top Tip: Get a copy of your records with them, if needed.

GOVERNMENT OFFICES

- ☐ Social Security Administration
- ☐ City/Province Tax Bureaus
- ☐ State/Federal Tax Bureaus
- ☐ Department of Motor Vehicles
- ☐ Voter Registration
- ☐ Veterans Administration
- ☐ _____
- ☐ _____

PERSONAL ACCOUNTS

- ☐ Employer's human resources department
- ☐ Pharmacy
- ☐ Dry cleaner
- ☐ Laundry service
- ☐ Lawn service
- ☐ Health club
- ☐ Other clubs or organizations where you are a member
- ☐ _____
- ☐ _____

Top Tip: Ask if you can transfer your membership, or if you have to cancel it.

UTILITIES

- ☐ Electricity
- ☐ Water
- ☐ Sewage
- ☐ Garbage
- ☐ Gas
- ☐ Telephone
- ☐ Internet

☐ Cable/Satellite/Pay TV

☐ _____

☐ _____

Top Tips:
- Ask for a "letter of reference" from the utility companies.
- Make sure utilities are still connected on your moving day(s).

MAIL AND PUBLICATIONS

☐ Post Office

☐ Newspaper

☐ Magazines

☐ Professional publications

☐ Newsletters

☐ _____

☐ _____

Top Tip: At the Post Office, ask for printed or online Change of Address forms.

FAMILY AND FRIENDS

☐ Prepare a list of their addresses (email – postal if you must)

☐ Send your new contact details

☐ _____

☐ _____

☐ _____

☐ _____

☐ _____

☐ _____

- [ ] _____
- [ ] _____
- [ ] _____
- [ ] _____
- [ ] _____
- [ ] _____
- [ ] _____
- [ ] _____
- [ ] _____
- [ ] _____
- [ ] _____
- [ ] _____
- [ ] _____
- [ ] _____
- [ ] _____
- [ ] _____
- [ ] _____
- [ ] _____
- [ ] _____
- [ ] _____
- [ ] _____
- [ ] _____
- [ ] _____
- [ ] _____
- [ ] _____
- [ ] _____
- [ ] _____
- [ ] _____
- [ ] _____
- [ ] _____
- [ ] _____
- [ ] _____

Appendix 2:

Checklists for your

International Relocation

International Relocation: Checklist 1

More than 2 Months before Moving

ORGANIZE YOUR PAPERWORK

☐ Open a new folder called *Relocation Folder* on your computer

☐ Create your (paper) *Moving File*

RESEARCH SCHOOLS IN NEW HOST CITY

☐ Decide on public or private school

☐ Research a school looking at:
   a) Students' school results and school's curriculum
   b) Facilities
   c) Fees
   d) Requirements

☐ Apply to school(s) on your short list

☐ _____

☐ _____

Top Tip: Many private schools have waiting lists. Enquire about them. To be on the safe side you can put your child's name down with several schools.

YOUR PET

- ☐ Research the rules and regulations for importing your pet into your new host country
- ☐ Contact the airline and ask your questions
- ☐ Arrange for your pet to be micro chipped
- ☐ Arrange the necessary vaccinations
- ☐ Ask for a pet passport
- ☐ Get a copy of your pet's veterinarian file
- ☐ Ask vet for tips for moving your pet
- ☐ Arrange air transport
- ☐ Organize customs clearing forms, etc.
- ☐ Book a kennel for quarantine
- ☐ _____
- ☐ _____

Top Tip: Many countries apply firm restrictions to pet immigration. Start this process as early as possible; just to be sure you won't have to leave your pet behind!

YOUR VACCINATIONS

- ☐ Research what vaccinations you need – or want – for your host country
- ☐ If applicable, organize vaccinations for each family member
- ☐ _____
- ☐ _____

Top Tips:
- Make sure your doctor issues a World Health Organization (WHO) International Certificate of Vaccinations.
- During the doctor's visit, ask for a copy of your medical documentation. It may be useful for your new doctor.

UPDATE YOUR PERSONAL DOCUMENTS

- ☐ Apply for or renew family members' passports
- ☐ Apply for visas for your new host country
- ☐ Renew drivers license, if needed
- ☐ Get an international drivers license, or a certified translation
- ☐ Get (unabridged) Birth Certificates
- ☐ Get Marriage Certificate
- ☐ Have a set of passport photos of each family member made
- ☐ _____
- ☐ _____

Top Tip: Find out what documents your new host country requires. Apply for or organize them early to allow enough time for official procedures.

FINANCES

Enquire about:

- ☐ Your pension plans
- ☐ Taxes (bilateral tax agreement; tax system in your new host country)
- ☐ Money transfer between countries
- ☐ _____
- ☐ _____

YOUR HOME

- ☐ Get in contact with real estate agent
- ☐ To recoup your bond: arrange for a property inspection
- ☐ Sell your house
- ☐ _____
- ☐ _____

International Relocation: Checklist 2

2 Months before Moving

CHOOSING AND DEALING WITH YOUR MOVING COMPANY

☐ Decide whether you're moving your household goods – or bring nothing to your new host country and purchase everything there

☐ Decide what services you need from your moving company:

a) truck rental

b) hiring movers for transport only

c) transport and packing of a part of your belongings by movers

d) transport and packing of all of your belongings by movers

e) transport, packing and additional services by movers

☐ Find out if your host country requires the packing be done by movers (e.g. USA: no self-packing allowed)

☐ Contact your employer; see if they are paying for your relocation

☐ If your employer is paying for your move, read their moving policy to find out what services you are entitled to

☐ Decide on your budget

- ☐ Decide what date you want to move (mid-week / mid month = less expensive and less busy)
- ☐ Add any important information like quotes and receipts to your *Moving File*
- ☐ Find contact details of moving companies:
  a) Ask friends for a recommendation, OR
  b) Google "moving company" + your area
- ☐ Research moving companies; look at previous customers' reviews
- ☐ Contact 3 moving companies to compare prices
- ☐ Ask them to inspect your home before they prepare a quote (if they need to pack; probably not needed if they only have to transport your belongings)
- ☐ Show the moving agent EVERYTHING that you need to be moved
- ☐ Mention if anything else, something that is not in your home, will be added
- ☐ Mention what they DON'T need to move because you are selling or giving it away
- ☐ Discuss the date you want to move
- ☐ Compare the quotes you get from the moving companies:
  a) price
  b) services offered
  c) conditions
  d) insurance offered
- ☐ Choose a moving company and sign the contract
- ☐ Keep the name, phone number and email address of your contact person with the moving company in your *Moving File* and save it in your mobile phone
- ☐ Inform the moving company about changes, for instance:
  a) additional items to be moved

b) items that you gave away or stored

c) change of moving date

☐ _____

☐ _____

Top Tip: If your friends help you moving, consider what you'll do in case somebody causes damage to one of your items or your home. Do your friends have insurance for such damages? Can you organize extra insurance for your moving day? Try not to let a damage ruin your friendship.

NOTICE

☐ Give notice at work

☐ Give notice to your landlord

☐ Give notice to your domestic or other employees

☐ Inform the school that you're moving away

☐ _____

☐ _____

PLACE YOU ARE MOVING TO

☐ Start researching the town/community you are moving to

☐ Make travel arrangements

☐ Arrange interim accommodation at your destination

☐ _____

☐ _____

COLLECT IMPORTANT DOCUMENTS

☐ Vaccination records, incl. World Health Organization (WHO) International Certificate of Vaccinations

☐ Medical prescriptions

- ☐ Medical documentation
- ☐ Dental file
- ☐ Ask doctor, dentist, etc. for referrals in your new host city
- ☐ School records and other recommended documents
- ☐ Veterinarian file
- ☐ Copies of financial records
- ☐ Copies of legal records
- ☐ Insurance: call your agent and ask if you need to make any changes to your policy, or even have to get a new insurance policy
- ☐ _____
- ☐ _____

SORT OUT ITEMS YOU MIGHT NOT BE ABLE TO TAKE WITH YOU

- ☐ Research your new host country's import restrictions (e.g. alcohol, DVDs, books, etc.)
- ☐ Organize permission to take unusual items abroad: guns, crocodile skin handbag (endangered species), etc.
- ☐ Sell or give away plants
- ☐ Get rid of explosive, corrosive or flammable items like fireworks, matches, cleaning fluids, acids, chemistry sets, aerosol cans, ammunition, paint and thinner, etc.
- ☐ Use up or discard poisons like weed-killer, fuel in your lawn mower, etc.
- ☐ Follow the instructions given by your moving company
- ☐ _____
- ☐ _____

MOVING YOUR CAR OR OTHER MOTOR VEHICLES

- ☐ Decide if you're taking or leaving your car or other motor vehicles
- ☐ If you want to take it, contact moving company
- ☐ Prepare documents
- ☐ Have your car serviced
- ☐ Follow instructions given by moving company
- ☐ _____
- ☐ _____

GO THROUGH YOUR BELONGINGS

- ☐ Create a floor plan of your new home and see if all your furniture fits in
- ☐ Note which items are too bulky for the new place
- ☐ Note which items will need special packing or extra insurance coverage
- ☐ _____
- ☐ _____

'SHRINK' YOUR HOUSEHOLD GOODS

- ☐ Eat the food in your fridge, freezer and pantry
- ☐ Finish the wine, beer and spirits you own
- ☐ Use up cosmetic supplies, cleaning agents and other household items
- ☐ Sort out your belongings (refer to book for tips)
- ☐ Organize storage facility
- ☐ Give items away to family and friends (house plants, books, etc.)
- ☐ Organize a garage sale
- ☐ Sell things via online auction service (e.g. eBay)

- ☐ Donate clothing, books, left over food, drinks, cleaning agents, etc. to charity
- ☐ _____
- ☐ _____

Top Tip: Ask the charity for receipts showing the items' approximate value – you might get a tax deduction

INVENTORY
- ☐ Ask your moving company for information about the inventory
- ☐ Write an inventory of the items that are to be shipped
- ☐ _____
- ☐ _____

FINANCES
- ☐ Cancel automated payments (e.g. rent, post box, levy, club memberships,)
- ☐ Settle any outstanding bills
- ☐ _____
- ☐ _____

International Relocation:
Checklist 3

1 Month before Moving

PREPARE THE FAMILY
☐ Make farewell visits to places with happy memories
☐ Organize a going-away party for your children
☐ Organize a going-away party for yourselves
☐ _____
☐ _____

IN AND AROUND YOUR HOME
☐ Return library books, DVDs, etc.
☐ Return borrowed, checked-out and rented items
☐ Get things back you have lent or rented out
☐ Make any home repairs you have committed to
☐ _____
☐ _____

UTILITIES, MAIL, ETC.
☐ Ask for utilities to be disconnected
(refer to *Change of Address – Moving Checklist*)
☐ Ask Post Office to forward your mail to your new address
☐ Ask neighbor to look out for mail after you moved
☐ Organize utilities to be connected in your new host city
☐ _____

Tip Tips:
- Schedule **disconnection** of services for 3 days **after your moving day** (allow for cleaning).
- Schedule **connection** of services in new city for 2 days **before your arrival day** (allow for inspection and/or cleaning).

INVENTORY OF HOUSEHOLD GOODS

☐ Finish your inventory

☐ _____

☐ _____

ORGANIZE PACKING MATERIAL

☐ Boxes

☐ Tape

☐ Bubble wrap

☐ Stuffing/padding

☐ Markers

☐ Dish barrels, if needed

☐ Wardrobe boxes, if needed

☐ _____

☐ _____

Top Tip: If you are using a moving company ask them to deliver the packing material now.

START PACKING

☐ If you are not allowed to pack your items by yourself: organize what you want to be together by putting them loosely into a box or on a pile

- ☐ Pack things you won't use in the next few weeks (like winter resp. summer clothes)
- ☐ Disassemble outdoor items like swing set, wendy house
- ☐ Take pictures of things you are about to disassemble
- ☐ Place all screws, bolts, brackets in small (Ziploc) plastic bags, and tape this to the disassembled item
- ☐ Start disassembling pre-fabricated furniture
- ☐ _____
- ☐ _____

PACKING BEST PRACTICE
- ☐ Label every box clearly (content, room to go)
- ☐ Write a number on the lid and the side of each box
- ☐ Use the number to prepare an inventory list of each box
- ☐ Note damages on furniture in your inventory list
- ☐ _____
- ☐ _____

WHITE GOODS ETC.
- ☐ Check moving instructions for washing machine etc.
- ☐ Organize a plumber to prepare it for transport
- ☐ Arrange for an expert to install fixtures upon your arrival in the new home, if needed
- ☐ _____
- ☐ _____

PETS, BULKY AND DIFFICULT ITEMS
- ☐ Arrange transport of pets
- ☐ Plan how to transport bulky items
- ☐ Plan how to transport difficult items
- ☐ _____

FINANCES

- ☐ Open bank accounts in your new host city
- ☐ Apply for Post Office box in your new host city
- ☐ Organize sufficient cash for the relocation
- ☐ Organize foreign currency
- ☐ Plan for tips for the movers
- ☐ Organize form of payment for moving company
- ☐ Pay deposit for moving company
- ☐ Notify credit card company that you'll be using credit cards abroad
- ☐ _____
- ☐ _____

CHANGE OF ADDRESS NOTIFICATIONS

- ☐ Organize inexpensive ways of staying in touch with family and friends
- ☐ Prepare emails for change of address notifications
- ☐ For addresses: see *Change of Address – Moving Checklist*
- ☐ Get 'change of address notifications' from Post Office for those without email address
- ☐ Prepare and send these
- ☐ _____
- ☐ _____

Top Tips:

- Organize inexpensive ways of staying in touch with friends and family, such as Skype, Viber, WhatsApp, Facetime, Google Chat, etc.
- Open accounts for yourself, and maybe also for your parents (who may not be so Internet savvy).
- Add the contact info to your 'change of address notifications'.

International Relocation: Checklist 4

3 Weeks before Moving

ORGANIZE HELPERS

☐ Babysitter for your kids for moving day

☐ Somebody to look after your pet on moving day

☐ Friends etc. as helpers for moving day

☐ Babysitter and helpers for moving-in day at your new home (if not the same day as moving day)

☐ _____

☐ _____

DAY OFF

☐ Notify employer you need a day off for moving

☐ _____

☐ _____

SCHOOL RECORDS

☐ Ask for school records to be forwarded to new school

☐ _____

☐ _____

CLEANING OF NEW HOME

☐ Confirm that your new home will be thoroughly cleaned

☐ If not sure, arrange to have it cleaned by somebody other than you before you move in

☐ _____

☐ _____

HIDING PLACES

☐ Empty secret hiding places for valuables
☐ Collect hidden spare house keys
☐ _____
☐ _____

START PREPARING YOUR SPECIAL BOXES:

Moving Day Box

☐ List the items you will need on moving day
☐ For instance: drinks, snacks, packing tape, scissors, markers, first aid kit, etc.
☐ Start collecting items and putting into this box, if not constantly in use
☐ Label the box DO NOT MOVE – MOVING DAY BOX
☐ Keep this box separated from other moving boxes
☐ _____
☐ _____

Trip Kit

☐ List the items you and your family will need while travelling
☐ For instance: passports, visa, pet's travel documents, marriage certificate, school records, prescription medicine, etc. (see Chapter 3)

- ☐ Add drinks and snacks, children's favorite toys and maybe a pillow, entertainment devices like iPad, mobile phone charger, sunglasses, dog's lead and bowl, foreign currency, etc.
- ☐ Start collecting items and putting into this box, if not constantly in use
- ☐ Label the box DO NOT MOVE – TRIP KIT
- ☐ Keep separated from other moving boxes
- ☐ _____
- ☐ _____

Survival Box
- ☐ List the first things you will need in your new home
- ☐ For instance: prescription medicine for a few weeks, toiletries, towels, bedding, flashlight, toilet paper, pet food, children's school needs, tea/coffee and UHT milk, electronic devices chargers, etc.
- ☐ Start collecting items and putting into this box, if not constantly in use
- ☐ Label the box DO NOT MOVE – SURVIVAL BOX
- ☐ Keep separated from other moving boxes
- ☐ _____
- ☐ _____

Valuables
- ☐ List your precious belongings
- ☐ Take pictures
- ☐ Organize storage, if needed (bank safe etc.)
- ☐ Plan how you will move them
- ☐ Make arrangements for their transport
- ☐ Take extra insurance coverage for the transport, if needed

☐ Keep them in a safe place, for instance: with neighbors or friends; locked in your car

☐ _____

☐ _____

Important Information About Your Home – For The Next Tenant / Owner

☐ Collect instruction manuals
☐ Collect other important information about your home
☐ Put them into this box
☐ Add your (new) contact details
☐ Label the box :
DO NOT MOVE – HOME INFORMATION
☐ Keep separated from other moving boxes

☐ _____

☐ _____

SELF-PACKERS

☐ Start serious packing

☐ _____

☐ _____

PACKING BEST PRACTICE

☐ Label every box clearly (content, room to go)
☐ Write a number on the lid and the side of each box
☐ Use the number to prepare an inventory list of each box
☐ Note damages on furniture in your inventory list

☐ _____

☐ _____

DISASSEMBLING BEST PRACTICE

- ☐ Take pictures of things you are about to disassemble
- ☐ Place all screws, bolts, brackets in small (Ziploc) plastic bags, and tape this to the disassembled item
- ☐ _____
- ☐ _____

FIXING

- ☐ Remove any fixtures you are taking with you
- ☐ Fix damages to the apartment / house
- ☐ _____
- ☐ _____

International Relocation: Checklist 5

1 Week before Moving

PAPERWORK

☐ Re-check that all paperwork for old and new place is complete

☐ _____

☐ _____

INTERNATIONAL TRANSFER

☐ Re-confirm travel arrangements for family

☐ Re-confirm travel arrangements for pets

☐ Prepare transfer of pets

☐ Re-confirm arrangements for your container

☐ Confirm parking for your moving container

☐ _____

☐ _____

PETS

☐ Buy your pet a collar

☐ Attach 2 identification tags to your pet's collar

☐ Write old contact details on one identification tag

☐ Write new contact details on the other identification tag

☐ _____

☐ _____

IN/AROUND YOUR HOME

☐ Plan how you will spend your last night in your old home

☐ Mow the lawn for the last time

☐ Clean the lawn mower and empty petrol and oil

☐ Empty garden hose

☐ Empty your locker at gym or club

☐ Collect dry cleaning

☐ _____

☐ _____

FOOD AND DRINKS

☐ Plan meals for the last days

☐ Completely finish the food in your freezer and pantry

☐ Organize food and drinks for moving day – including helper and packers

☐ _____

☐ _____

SUITCASES

☐ Pack a suitcase for each family member

☐ Add enough clothes to wear for a few days/weeks

☐ Add personal items

☐ _____

☐ _____

KEEP THESE SEPARATED FROM YOUR OTHER MOVING BOXES

☐ *Moving Day Box*

☐ *Trip Kit*

- ☐ *Survival Box*
- ☐ *Valuables*
- ☐ *Important information about your home*
- ☐ _____
- ☐ _____

Top Tip: Keep these boxes, as well as the suitcases, in a (empty) bathroom. Stick a note onto the bathroom door: DO NOT TAKE ANY BOXES IN HERE.
Close the door on moving day.

SELF-PACKERS
- ☐ Keep packing
- ☐ Clean shelves, cupboards, etc. when they are empty
- ☐ _____
- ☐ _____

ELECTRONICS
- ☐ Back up your computer hard drive
- ☐ Secure back-up (Cloud? *Valuables* box?); don't pack it into same box as computer
- ☐ Take photos of cables
- ☐ Unplug electronics at least 24 hours before packing
- ☐ Disassemble and carefully pack
- ☐ Add remote controls
- ☐ _____
- ☐ _____

VALUABLES
- ☐ Empty your safe deposit box
- ☐ Secure these items for safe travel

☐ _____

☐ _____

PLAN OF NEW HOME

☐ Draw a plan of your new home

☐ Draw furniture on it, so moving company knows where to place them

☐ _____

☐ _____

International Relocation: Checklist 6

Change of Address List

WHO NEEDS TO KNOW ABOUT YOUR RELOCATION

PROFESSIONAL SERVICES

- ☐ Doctors
- ☐ Dentists
- ☐ Insurance agent
- ☐ Lawyer
- ☐ Accountant
- ☐ Bank
- ☐ Broker
- ☐ Credit Card company
- ☐ Auto Finance company
- ☐ Veterinarian
- ☐ _____
- ☐ _____

Top Tip: Get a copy of your records from them, if needed.

GOVERNMENT OFFICES

- ☐ Social Security Administration
- ☐ City/Province Tax Bureaus
- ☐ State/Federal Tax Bureaus
- ☐ Department of Motor Vehicles
- ☐ Voter Registration
- ☐ Veterans Administration
- ☐ _____
- ☐ _____

PERSONAL ACCOUNTS

- ☐ Employer's human resources department
- ☐ Pharmacy
- ☐ Dry cleaner
- ☐ Laundry service
- ☐ Lawn service
- ☐ Health club
- ☐ Other clubs or organizations where you are a member
- ☐ _____
- ☐ _____

Top Tip: Ask if you can transfer your membership or if you have to cancel it.

UTILITIES

- ☐ Electricity
- ☐ Water
- ☐ Sewage
- ☐ Garbage
- ☐ Gas
- ☐ Telephone
- ☐ Internet

☐   Cable/Satellite/Pay TV
☐   _____
☐   _____

Top Tips:
-   Ask for a "letter of reference" from the utility companies.
-   Make sure utilities are still connected on your moving day(s).

MAIL AND PUBLICATIONS
☐   Post Office
☐   Newspaper
☐   Magazines
☐   Professional publications
☐   Newsletters
☐   _____
☐   _____

   Top Tip: At the Post Office, ask for printed or online Change of Address forms.

FAMILY AND FRIENDS
☐   Prepare a list of their addresses (email – postal if you must)
☐   Send your new contact details
☐   _____
☐   _____
☐   _____
☐   _____
☐   _____
☐   _____

- ☐ _____
- ☐ _____
- ☐ _____
- ☐ _____
- ☐ _____
- ☐ _____
- ☐ _____
- ☐ _____
- ☐ _____
- ☐ _____
- ☐ _____
- ☐ _____
- ☐ _____
- ☐ _____
- ☐ _____
- ☐ _____
- ☐ _____
- ☐ _____
- ☐ _____
- ☐ _____
- ☐ _____
- ☐ _____
- ☐ _____
- ☐ _____
- ☐ _____
- ☐ _____
- ☐ _____
- ☐ _____
- ☐ _____
- ☐ _____
- ☐ _____

Made in the USA
Las Vegas, NV
07 March 2022

45186113R00069